Cultural Cuisine

PHO

by Richard Sebra

abdobooks.com

Published by Pop!, a division of ABDO, PO Box 398166,
Minneapolis, Minnesota 55439. Copyright © 2021 by POP, LLC.
International copyrights reserved in all countries. No part
of this book may be reproduced in any form without written
permission from the publisher. Pop!™ is a trademark and logo
of POP, LLC.

Printed in the United States of America, North Mankato,
Minnesota.

082020
012021

THIS BOOK CONTAINS
RECYCLED MATERIALS

Cover Photo: iStockphoto
Interior Photos: iStockphoto, 1, 6, 7, 11, 12–13, 14, 20, 21, 22,
29; Shutterstock Images, 5, 9, 18–19, 25, 26–27, 28; Shaun
Higson/Vietnam - Hanoi/Alamy, 10; Red Line Editorial, 15;
BrownWCannonIII/Cannon Photography LLC/Alamy, 17

Editor: Sophie Geister-Jones
Series Designers: Candice Keimig, Victoria Bates, and Laura
Graphenteen

Library of Congress Control Number: 2019954989
Publisher's Cataloging-in-Publication Data

Names: Sebra, Richard, author.

Title: Pho / by Richard Sebra

Description: Minneapolis, Minnesota : POP!, 2021 | Series:
Cultural cuisine | Includes online resources and index.

Identifiers: ISBN 9781532167782 (lib. bdg.) | ISBN 9781532168888
(ebook)

Subjects: LCSH: Vietnamese cooking--Juvenile literature.
| Noodle soups--Juvenile literature. | Ethnic food--
Juvenile literature. | International cooking--Juvenile
literature. | Food--Social aspects--Juvenile literature.

Classification: DDC 641.59597--dc23

WELCOME TO
DiscoverRoo!

Pop open this book and you'll find QR codes loaded
with information, so you can learn even more!

Scan this code* and others like
it while you read, or visit the
website below to make this
book pop!

popbooksonline.com/pho

*Scanning QR codes requires a web-enabled smart device with a QR code reader app and a camera.

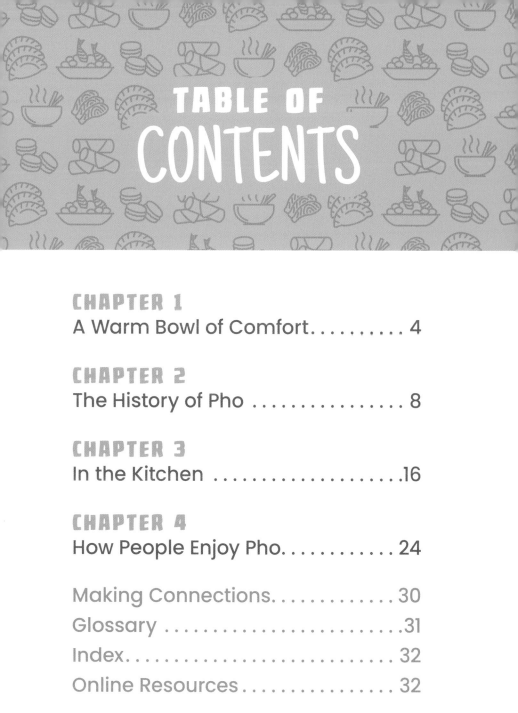

TABLE OF CONTENTS

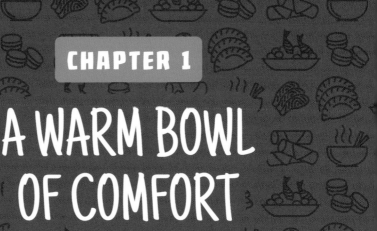

CHAPTER 1

A WARM BOWL OF COMFORT

It is early morning. But throughout Vietnam, people are already awake. Pots of beef **broth** sit on stoves. They have been **simmering** all night. In one home, a cook puts noodles, beef, and

WATCH A VIDEO HERE!

People in Vietnam often buy pho from street vendors.

vegetables in a bowl. She pours the broth

over them. The steaming soup is ready

to serve.

Pho is a noodle soup. It is made with broth, meat, rice noodles, and vegetables. Pho came from North Vietnam. But the soup became popular all over the country.

DID YOU KNOW?

Pho is pronounced "fuh."

Pho made with beef is called pho bo.

CHAPTER 2
THE HISTORY OF PHO

Pho first appeared in the early 1900s.

A few Vietnamese towns claim to have

invented it. Nobody knows which town

served it first. But people agree that pho

is from northern Vietnam.

LEARN MORE HERE!

Many people consider pho the national dish of Vietnam.

When the French took over cities in Vietnam, they built buildings in European styles.

In the mid-1800s, France took over Vietnam. The French made the area a **colony**. French people who lived there made a beef **stew**. The stew was called pot-au-feu. Some people think this dish was the basis for pho.

Pot-au-feu is made with beef and vegetables such as carrots and celery.

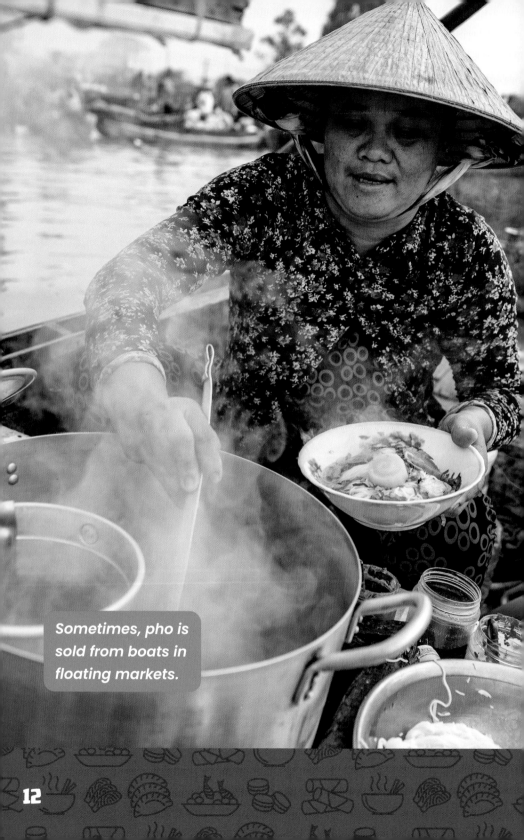

Sometimes, pho is sold from boats in floating markets.

Vietnamese people began making their own beef **broth**. Then they added noodles. Street vendors carried **simmering** pots of broth on wooden poles. They served bowls for people as they walked. Pho started to appear in restaurants in the 1930s and 1940s.

In 1954, Vietnam split into North Vietnam and South Vietnam. Many people in the North were afraid of the North's new government. They fled to South Vietnam. These people brought pho with them. Pho took on new flavors in the South. People added herbs and sauces.

DIVIDED VIETNAM (1954—1975)

In the 1950s, North and South Vietnam went to war. The North defeated the South in 1975. Many people were forced to leave Vietnam. A lot of them went to the United States.

LAOS

THAILAND

CAMBODIA

DEMILITARIZED ZONE

NORTH VIETNAM
SOUTH VIETNAM

N
W E
S

CHAPTER 3

IN THE KITCHEN

Pho **broth** takes a long time to make.

First, the cook adds beef bones to a big

pot of water. The cook lets the bones

and water **simmer**. Then the cook adds

spices. The broth simmers for several

TRY A RECIPE HERE!

Some pho broth takes more than 24 hours to make.

more hours. Then the cook **strains** it.

This step makes the broth smooth.

The cook boils the rice noodles
in another pot. The cooked noodles go
in the bottom of a soup bowl. The cook
places thin slices of raw beef on top.
Onions and scallions are often added to
the bowl.

People assemble each bowl of pho separately.

Then the cook pours boiling-hot
broth in the bowl. The hot broth cooks
the meat.

Many people eat pho with chopsticks and a spoon.

People can add toppings to their pho.

Lime, Thai basil, and pepper are popular

toppings. Some people add bean sprouts

too. Toppings are sprinkled over the soup.

Some people eat pho with hot sauce on

the side.

Additions to the dish are often served alongside pho.

RECIPE CHECKLIST

PHO INGREDIENTS

- 3 yellow onions
- 4-inch piece of ginger
- 5 pounds beef soup bones
- 5 star anise
- 6 whole cloves
- 3-inch cinnamon stick
- 1 pound beef cut into 2-inch pieces
- 1 1/2 tablespoons salt
- 1 ounce yellow rock sugar
- 4 tablespoons fish sauce

- 1 1/2 pounds rice noodles
- 1/2 pound thinly sliced steak
- 3 scallions
- 1/3 cup chopped cilantro
- ground black pepper

Makes 8 servings

INSTRUCTIONS

1. Roast two onions and the ginger. Then remove their skins and set aside.

2. Boil the beef bones for three minutes. Then dump out the liquid and rinse the bones.

3. Place the bones back in the pot and fill with water. Add cooked onions and ginger, as well as spices, beef, salt, sugar, and fish sauce.

4. Let the pot boil for 1.5 hours.

5. Remove the beef and cook for three more hours. Then strain the broth.

6. Boil the rice noodles and place them in serving bowls.

7. Place the thin slices of raw steak in each bowl.

8. Then add fresh sliced onion, scallions, cilantro, and pepper.

9. Pour boiling-hot broth in each bowl.

10. Wait 30 seconds for the steak to cook.

CHAPTER 4

HOW PEOPLE ENJOY PHO

Pho can be eaten at any time of day.

In Vietnam, pho is often enjoyed

at breakfast. The weather in Vietnam is

usually very hot. But the morning is a little

cooler. It's a great time for hot soup.

COMPLETE AN ACTIVITY HERE!

Some pho shops sell out before ten o'clock in the morning.

After the 1960s and 1970s, many

Vietnamese people fled to the United

States. They brought pho to their new

home. The first pho restaurant in the

United States opened in 1980. It was

in the Little Saigon neighborhood of

Orange County, California. Since then,

pho has grown popular around the world.

Seafood pho may contain shrimp, crab, or octopus.

Beef pho is the most popular version.

But pho can be made with chicken or

seafood. Today, there are many types

of pho. Some have less **broth**. Others use different meats or spices.

For vegetarians, pho can be made with tofu instead of meat.

TEXT-TO-SELF

Would you want to try cooking pho? Why or why not?

TEXT-TO-TEXT

Have you read books about other kinds of soup? How are they similar to or different from pho?

TEXT-TO-WORLD

Pho was first made in Vietnam, but now people all around the world enjoy it. What other foods have spread to new places?

broth — a liquid cooked with meat or vegetables.

colony — a land taken over or ruled by another country.

simmer — to boil very gently at a low temperature.

stew — a thick soup usually containing meat and vegetables.

strain — to separate solid pieces from a liquid.

INDEX

ONLINE RESOURCES

popbooksonline.com

Scan this code* and others like it while you read, or visit the website below to make this book pop!

popbooksonline.com/pho

*Scanning QR codes requires a web-enabled smart device with a QR code reader app and a camera.